Contents

Lesson 1 Planning for Success

Exercise A Complete the sentences. Use the simple past or present perfect of the verb below the line. The first two questions are done as examples.

Remember?

The present perfect (*have/has* + past participle) tells about an action that started in the past and continues into the present.

The simple past tense tells about an action that was started and ended in the past.

1. Patria and her grandmother _____have done_____ many
   projects together.
   _{do}

2. While they _____worked_____, they _____talked_____
   _{work}   _{talk}
   about life.

3. Patria _____ many things about her grandmother's life from their talks.
   _{learn}

4. Her grandmother _____ to the US from Puerto Rico many years ago.
   _{come}

5. Since that time, she _____ her goal of building a life for herself and her family.
   _{accomplish}

6. Life in the US was not what she _____ it to be like.
   _{imagine}

7. She _____ her goals by working hard.
   _{achieve}

Exercise B Answer these questions. Write complete sentences.

1. How long have you lived in the US?

   _____

2. How long have you studied English?

   _____

3. What special goal have you dreamed of? How long have you dreamed of it?

   _____

4. What have you done to achieve your goal?

   _____

5. Who have you asked for help in achieving this goal?

   _____

WORKBOOK 4

English
No Problem!

Kathryn Quinones
Office of Adult and Continuing Education
New York City Department of Education, NY

Donna Korol
Office of Adult and Continuing Education
New York City Department of Education, NY

New Readers Press

English—No Problem!™
English—No Problem! Level 4 Workbook
ISBN 1-56420-364-6

Copyright © 2004 New Readers Press
New Readers Press
Division of ProLiteracy Worldwide
1320 Jamesville Avenue, Syracuse, New York 13210
www.newreaderspress.com

Printed in the United States of America
9 8 7 6 5 4 3 2

All proceeds from the sale of New Readers Press materials
support literacy programs in the United States and worldwide.

Acquisitions Editor: Paula L. Schlusberg
Developer: Mendoza and Associates
Project Director: Roseanne Mendoza
Project Editor: Pat Harrington-Wydell
Content Editor: Judi Lauber
Production Director: Heather Witt-Badoud
Designer: Kimbrly Koennecke
Illustrations: Carolyn Boehmer, Steve Ryan
Production Specialist: Jeffrey R. Smith
Cover Design: Kimbrly Koennecke
Cover Photography: Robert Mescavage Photography
Photo Credits: Hal Silverman Studio

Exercise C Match the words and their definitions. The first one is done as an example. Then write a sentence with each word in your notebook.

_d_ **1.** form a picture in your mind   a. predict

_____ **2.** make clear   b. accomplish

_____ **3.** what is   c. clarify

_____ **4.** say what will happen in the future   d. imagine

_____ **5.** finish, complete   e. reality

Exercise D Read the following story. Then answer the questions. If the story does not answer the question, write *no information*. The first question is done as an example.

Ivan Postman has dreamed of discovering a cure for the common cold since he was 10 years old. He has lived in the frozen Arctic for his entire life, and he has had a cold every year since he was born. He has read over 500 books about the common cold. He has asked a famous botanist for information about herbs and natural medicine. He still hasn't achieved the outcome he wanted, but Ivan has accomplished one important thing: He has found a job in Florida!

1. How long has Ivan lived in the US?

no information

2. How long has he studied English?

_____

3. What special goal has he dreamed of achieving? How long has this been his dream?

_____

_____

4. What has he done to achieve his goal?

_____

5. Who has he asked for help in achieving his goal?

_____

_____

Lesson 2 Learning from the Past

Exercise A   Use the words in bold type to answer the questions below. Write complete sentences.

1. What is one long-term goal that you want to **accomplish** this year?

   _____

2. What is one **event** that you would like to attend this year?

   _____

3. What is one thing that you haven't **dared** to do but would like to try?

   _____

4. What is one dream that you have **fulfilled** in your life?

   _____

5. What is one **experience** that you have liked very much this year?

   _____

In-Class Extension   Share your sentences about goals with your classmates. Good luck achieving your goals.

Exercise B   Read this letter to Patria from her friend Jack. In your notebook, make a chart of the verbs he used in the simple past, the present perfect, and the past perfect tenses. Be sure to look for long forms and contractions.

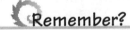

Remember?

The past perfect (*had* + past participle) shows an action that was completed before another action in the past.

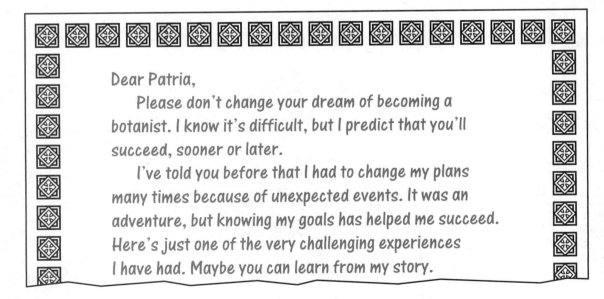

Dear Patria,
   Please don't change your dream of becoming a botanist. I know it's difficult, but I predict that you'll succeed, sooner or later.
   I've told you before that I had to change my plans many times because of unexpected events. It was an adventure, but knowing my goals has helped me succeed. Here's just one of the very challenging experiences I have had. Maybe you can learn from my story.

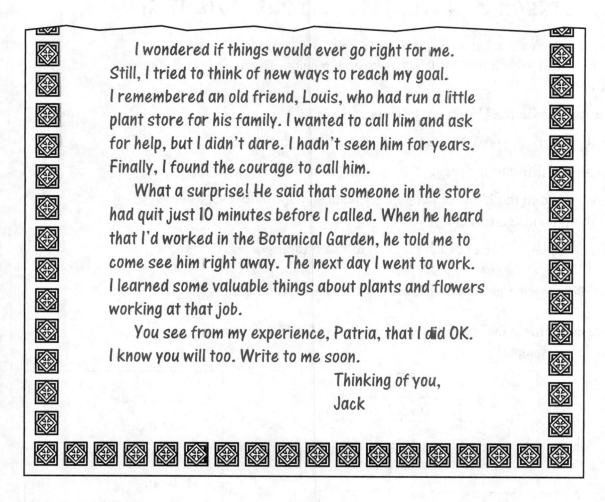

I wondered if things would ever go right for me. Still, I tried to think of new ways to reach my goal. I remembered an old friend, Louis, who had run a little plant store for his family. I wanted to call him and ask for help, but I didn't dare. I hadn't seen him for years. Finally, I found the courage to call him.

What a surprise! He said that someone in the store had quit just 10 minutes before I called. When he heard that I'd worked in the Botanical Garden, he told me to come see him right away. The next day I went to work. I learned some valuable things about plants and flowers working at that job.

You see from my experience, Patria, that I did OK. I know you will too. Write to me soon.

Thinking of you,
Jack

Exercise C   Read the letter again carefully. As you read, think about things that Jack's experience can teach you. Then follow these steps:

- **Brainstorm.** Take notes in the circles.

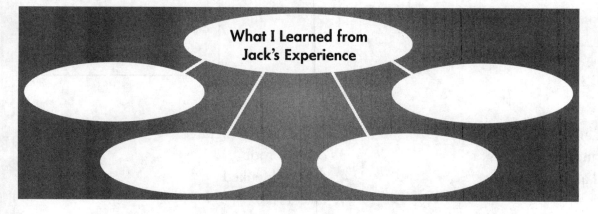

What I Learned from Jack's Experience

- **Organize your notes.** Write a paragraph in your notebook. Begin the paragraph like this: "Jack's challenging experience has taught me the following things: . . ."

- **Present.** Show your paragraph to your teacher.

Lesson 3 Living Up to Your Potential

Exercise A   Read the sentences below. Some of these statements are facts. Others are opinions. Write *F* next to each fact. Write *O* next to each opinion. The first question is done as an example.

___F___ **1.** Most workers in the US do not have farm jobs.

_____ **2.** You should try to speak English, even if it isn't perfect.

_____ **3.** English is a difficult language.

_____ **4.** Many people in the US take personality tests and aptitude tests to help them choose a career.

_____ **5.** In the US, people need perfect English to reach their goals.

In-Class Extension   Discuss your answers with group members. Do you all agree?

Exercise B   Use the words in the box to fill in the crossword puzzle. One word has been filled in as an example.

accomplish

aptitude

dare

✔ dream

frustrated

imagine

personality

profession

stuck

Across

5. hope

6. qualities of an individual

7. not able to move

8. interest and ability

Down

1. achieve

2. dream about, picture

3. career or job

4. feeling blocked

9. take a risk

Exercise C In the US, people usually choose their own jobs. In some countries, however, children often do the same work as their parents. The chart below lists some reasons people choose a job. If you think of other reasons, add them to the chart.

Think about whether each reason is good or bad. For each good reason, check the *Good* column. For each bad reason, check the *Bad* column. If a reason is sometimes good and sometimes bad, check the *Maybe* column.

One Step Up
For every "Maybe" you checked, write sentences describing two situations—a situation when the reason is good and one when the reason is bad.

Reasons Why People Choose a Job	Good	Bad	Maybe
to follow a parent's example			✔
to do something they like			
to try to make a lot of money			
because a career counselor recommended it			
to work where others speak their language			
Other:			
Other:			

In-Class Extension Compare your chart with other students' charts. Discuss any differences. Why do you think as you do?

Exercise D Write a paragraph about how you chose a job. Then revise and edit your paragraph.

Ask yourself, "Is the sentence order logical?" If not, use arrows and circles to show how you will change the order when you rewrite your paragraph. Then do these things:

- Take out three words that aren't really necessary.
- Add two words that make your paragraph more interesting.
- Add one more detail.
- Check your vocabulary. Have you used new words from this unit? If not, add some.
- Check your spelling, punctuation, and capitalization carefully.

When you finish, rewrite your paragraph. Give it to your teacher.

One Step Up
Use a magnet to hang your time line and letter from page 17 in your student book on your refrigerator. Look at them each time you open the refrigerator. Do something every day to reach your goals.

Looking at Your Goals Think about your goals for this unit.

How well can you . . .	Not very well		Somewhat		Very well
identify your most important goals?	1	2	3	4	5
make a plan for reaching your goals?	1	2	3	4	5
use problem-solving techniques?	1	2	3	4	5
use the past perfect, present perfect, and simple past?	1	2	3	4	5
use appropriate intonation with questions and statements?	1	2	3	4	5
another goal: _____	1	2	3	4	5

Learning about Setting Goals Think back on the lessons. What was the most important thing you learned about setting goals?

_____

_____

What do you still need to learn about setting and reaching your goals? List one or two things.

_____

_____

Improving Your English In this unit you studied these areas of English. Check the ones that have improved.

_____ understanding goal-setting words

_____ understanding problem-solving words

_____ using the simple past tense appropriately

_____ using the present perfect appropriately

_____ using the past perfect appropriately

_____ using correct intonation with statements

_____ using correct intonation with *yes/no* questions

_____ listening for information in a conversation

_____ reading a time line

_____ evaluating opinions in letters

_____ reading and writing opinions about personal development courses

_____ _____

another thing that you improved

Lesson 1 With a Little Help from My Friends

Exercise A Think about the people in your network. In your notebook, list names in a chart like the one below.

My Network

School	Home	Community	Other

Exercise B In your notebook, write sentences about yourself and the people you listed in Exercise A. Who would you ask for advice? Here is an example:

If I needed advice on cooking, I'd talk to my friend Helga.

Exercise C Complete this paragraph. Use the words from the box. The first blank is filled in as an example.

advice	challenge	network	professional	✔resume	skills

When you complete your _____resume_____, check it carefully. Be
₁
sure that you have included all of your _____ and abilities.
₂
Give it to people in your _____ to read. Ask them for
₃
_____ on ways to improve it. Copy your resume on good
₄
quality paper so that it looks _____. Creating a good
₅
resume can be a _____, but you can do it.
₆

Exercise D Unscramble the sentences and add punctuation. There may be more than one correct answer. The first sentence is done as an example.

1. to sell / with Ms. Patterson / some of my work / If my meeting / she'll try / goes well tomorrow

   If my meeting goes well tomorrow with Ms. Patterson, she'll try to sell
   some of my work.

2. these photos / look more professional / If I had / I could make / more time

   _____

3. look better / a little color / So do you think / to the photos / if I added / they would

   _____

Exercise E   Circle the correct words. Then copy the paragraph in your notebook. The first word is circled as an example.

If you are looking for a job, follow this | **1.** shyness   tone   (advice) | from Hassam, the cabdriver/painter. Give copies of your resume to people in your | **2.** skill   network   professional | . Practice interviewing with friends. Don't let negative feelings like | **3.** tense   tone   worry | and | **4.** emotions   ability   shyness | stop you from reaching your goal. Try to develop new | **5.** skills   resume   network | to improve your chances of finding a job. Try to make the | **6.** network   tone   tense | of your voice confident and friendly.

Exercise F   Match the beginnings and ends of the sentences. The first one is done as an example.

<u>c</u> **1.** I wouldn't worry about my interview   a. I would improve my pronunciation.

_____ **2.** If I watched more TV in English,   b. I wouldn't feel tense in social situations.

_____ **3.** I would make fewer mistakes   c. if I had more confidence.

_____ **4.** If I understood customs in the US,   d. if I listened to the advice of other people.

Now write the sentences, reversing the order of the clauses. Be sure to use a comma after an *if* clause. The first sentence is done as an example.

1. _____If I had more confidence, I wouldn't worry about my interview._____

2. _____

3. _____

4. _____

Exercise G   Complete these sentences. Use *would* in every sentence.

1. If I needed to improve my English quickly, _____

_____

2. If I found a wallet with $1,000 in it, _____

_____

3. If I were president of the US, _____

_____

Lesson 2 What Do I Do Now?

Exercise A Some business customs are appropriate in other countries but may be misunderstood in the US. Read the list of business customs in the chart below. Check the *OK* column if the custom is acceptable in the US. Check the *Not OK* column if it isn't. Check the *Not Sure* column if you don't know. Next, think of two more things that people do at business meetings in your home country. Add them to the chart. Check the appropriate column for each custom.

appropriate = right

acceptable = OK

misunderstand = get the wrong idea

Business Customs

At business meetings in some countries, a person might	At business meetings in the US, this behavior is		
	OK	Not OK	Not Sure
hug the other person			
bring a gift			
shake hands			
sit first			
make a joke			
wear a bright, colorful suit			
make eye contact			

One Step Up
Ask family members or friends what they think about the customs in the chart. Don't show them your answers until they give you theirs. Are their answers the same as yours? If not, why do you think they are different?

Exercise B Complete the sentences. Use the phrases from the box.

| go well | how to handle | in the eye | just in time | make a good impression |

1. Hassam got lost on the way to his interview, but he wasn't late. He was

   _____ .

2. He didn't _____ when he thought Ms. Patterson was

   the receptionist.

3. He didn't know _____ shaking hands and sitting down.

4. Fortunately things started to _____ when Hassam

   showed Ms. Patterson samples of his work.

5. Hassam looked Ms. Patterson _____ , smiled, and said

   "Thank you" at the end of the interview.

Exercise C   Think about a meeting that you attended recently. What do you remember about it? Organize your thoughts in an idea map like the one below.

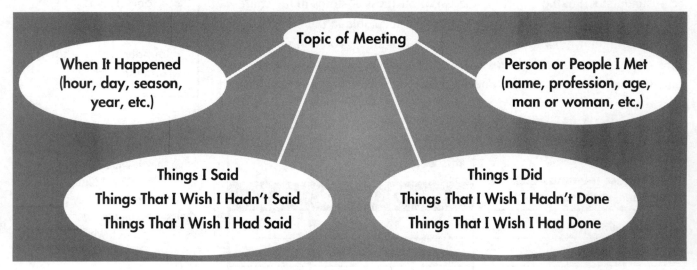

Now write a four-paragraph story about your meeting. Write one paragraph about the information that you put in each large circle. Then edit and revise your story:

- Does the order of the paragraphs make sense?
- Does the order of the sentences in each paragraph make sense?

If the answer is no, move pieces around. Use arrows and circles to show how you will change the order. Then do these things:

- Take out unnecessary words.
- Add words to make your story more interesting or give more details.
- Check your vocabulary. Have you used words correctly?
- Check your spelling, punctuation, and capitalization carefully.

Exercise D   This paragraph will help you review sentence stress. Underline the content words. Check your work with your teacher. Then read the paragraph aloud. Stress the content words by making them a little longer (not louder) than the other words.

Hassam was <u>confused</u> by Ms. Patterson's <u>body language</u>. When she held out her hand, he didn't remember the custom for greeting women at business meetings in the US. Ms. Patterson seemed annoyed when he didn't shake her hand. He really felt embarrassed. Hassam needed to learn about formal and informal greetings in the US before his next business meeting.

Lesson 3 Getting the Word Out

Exercise A Read the story below that Masa wrote for her English class. As you read, underline the words from the box on the right. One word has been underlined as an example.

My husband, Hassam, is an artist and a taxi driver. He drives a taxi during the day just to pay the bills. He paints in the evenings and on weekends. When Hassam asked me to help him prepare for an interview, I was happy to help him. Whenever I need help, he helps me too. It was my idea to network. This isn't a <u>custom</u> in my country, but I like it. Hassam called Peter, asking for advice, and Peter offered to come over to see his work. He told Hassam how to act more professionally in an interview. He looked at examples of Hassam's work. He was impressed with Hassam's abilities. I know Hassam will be successful. He has talent. He has a good plan for presenting himself and his paintings. He has confidence in his work, but he doesn't brag. He also has a good network, including his very smart, very skilled, *very* special wife!

After you finish reading, do the following things:

- Write each word you underlined in your notebook.
- In a dictionary, find a synonym for each word.
- Write the synonym beside each word. Here is an example:

custom = habit
_____

After you find synonyms for all the words, rewrite the story in your notebook. Substitute the synonyms for the original words, like this:

This isn't a habit in my country.
_____

Exercise B In your notebook, write three sentences about selling your skills. See how many vocabulary words from the unit you can use. Circle those words. In class, compare with a group member. Who used the most vocabulary words? Here is an example:

I can (advertise) my (abilities) with a good (resume).

Exercise C As you read the story below, underline examples of indirect speech. One example has been underlined for you. There are five more examples in the story.

I thought the young woman who greeted me was the receptionist, so I asked her to tell Ms. Patterson that I was there. I was embarrassed when <u>she said that *she* was Ms. Patterson.</u> She held out her hand, and I looked at it. Then I realized that she expected me to shake hands. I asked her if she wanted to see some pictures of my work. She looked a little annoyed and said that we should sit down first. I got even more confused then. I didn't think that I should sit down before she did, but she was pointing at the chair. Finally, I just sat down. I thought that I should say something, so I asked how she liked the weather. She folded her arms and frowned. It was easy to read that body language! She asked if I had a resume and photos. Luckily, I had my photos. After that, I relaxed. She said that my work was excellent and well-organized.

In your notebook, rewrite the five sentences that you underlined. Use quotation marks. Follow the example below. Notice the change from *she* to *I* in the example.

She said, "I am Ms. Patterson."

Exercise D In the word search puzzle, find the words listed in the box. They can be written forward or backward, across, down, or diagonally. Circle each word. One has been circled as an example. In your notebook, write a sentence using each word.

brag	✔confused	custom	embarrassed	shyness	talent	tone

```
X W B P T M N Y C E M D P S H
M B G G O R F D S E P U V S A
E Y Y T N A R H E U E T X E X
C B S W E K R Y J S J X R N T
K U R D M E G W V G U H C Y Q
C A K A T A L E N T S F K H R
W R L A G M Q M O Z G L N S I
O G P F X M L E B H K C X O D
Z G B D E S S A R R A B M E C
```

Looking at Your Goals Think about your goals for this unit.

How well can you . . .	Not very well		Somewhat		Very well
network to deal with challenges?	1	2	3	4	5
present yourself in English in a job interview?	1	2	3	4	5
understand everyday conversation?	1	2	3	4	5
ask for and give advice?	1	2	3	4	5
talk about your skills or your work?	1	2	3	4	5
another goal:_____	1	2	3	4	5

Learning about Networking Think back on the lessons. What was the most important thing you learned about networking and interviewing?

_____

_____

What do you still need to learn about networking and interviewing? List one or two things.

_____

_____

Improving Your English In this unit you studied these areas of English. Check the ones that have improved.

_____ understanding interview words

_____ understanding words for feelings

_____ saying vowel sounds in *say, said,* and *says*

_____ using indirect speech

_____ understanding the conditional contrary to fact

_____ stressing content words in sentences

_____ understanding how a speaker feels

_____ reading for sequence

_____ finding the main idea in a flyer

_____ reading and writing about US business customs

_____ _____
another thing that you improved

Lesson 1 Sharing Your Problems

Exercise A Circle the correct words. Then copy the story in your notebook.

Anna talks to her co-workers about her [**1.** dilemma   protection   barrier]

with Erin. Anna needs to develop a new [**2.** protection   issue   strategy]

for [**3.** protection   communicating   neglecting] with her. Anna wants to

[**4.** ignore   confront   cope] Erin about Mark. She is afraid that Mark is

[**5.** abuse   abusive   abuser] and [**6.** violence   violent   violate]. Anna

doesn't know how to [**7.** cope   neglect   ignore] with her fears. She can't

[**8.** issue   abuse   ignore] them, but she doesn't want to create more

[**9.** barriers   strategies   protections]. Anna's co-workers want her to get

[**10.** strategy   protection   violence] for Erin. They are a good

[**11.** issue   strategy   resource] for help. They think her

[**12.** issues   barriers   strategies] with Erin are serious. They don't want

Anna to [**13.** neglect   cope   abuse] her responsibility as a parent.

Exercise B Complete the sentences with the correct prepositions from the box.
You may use a preposition more than once. Some sentences have more than one
correct answer. The first sentence is done as an example.

at	during	for	✔in	next	on	to	with

1. Erin saw the hole _____ *in* _____ her tire.

2. She looked _____ the car.

3. Mark waited _____ her _____ his apartment.

4. Anna lost her temper _____ the conversation.

5. Erin stayed _____ her room _____ her bed.

6. The counselor sat _____ to Erin.

7. Erin asked _____ some advice _____ her situation.

8. Anna's friends spoke _____ caution.

9. Anna talked _____ her friends _____ the cafeteria
_____ one hour.

Exercise C Look at the picture of Anna and her friends in the cafeteria at work.

Describe the picture using prepositional phrases. Write as many sentences as possible in your notebook. Circle the prepositional phrases. Here is an example:

Anna is talking(_with her friends._)

In-Class Extension Share your sentences with your classmates. Ask them to identify the prepositional phrases.

Exercise D Match the phrases and their meanings.

_____ **1.** give up   a. listen; try to understand

_____ **2.** lose control   b. stop trying

_____ **3.** pay attention   c. be unable to behave calmly

Exercise E Complete the paragraph. Use the phrases from the box.

lose control	give up	pay attention

Erin doesn't want to _____ and stop seeing her

                                          1

boyfriend, Mark. He's usually nice and fun, but when he drinks, he can

_____. He becomes abusive and violent. Erin needs to

                       2

_____ to Mark's behavior.

                       3

Exercise F Write your own sentence for each vocabulary word below.

1. (confront) _____

2. (dilemma) _____

3. (ignore) _____

4. (protection) _____

5. (communicate) _____

6. (violent) _____

7. (cope) _____

8. (resource) _____

Lesson 2 Identifying Resources

Exercise A Add prepositional phrases to the sentences below. Use prepositions from the box. The first sentence is done as an example.

about	at	in	on	with
around	between	of	to	

1. Anna wanted to speak.

    Anna wanted to speak to Erin about Mark. _____

2. Anna knocked.

    _____

3. Erin was crying.

    _____

4. Anna told Erin to stop seeing Mark.

    _____

5. Erin was too angry to talk.

    _____

Exercise B Match the parts of the sentences. Then write the complete sentences in your notebook.

_____ **1.** Erin accused Mark   a. when he became angry.

_____ **2.** She encouraged him to   b. her mother was too protective.

_____ **3.** Mark was resentful of   c. of being an alcoholic.

_____ **4.** Erin was terrified of Mark   d. that she would help her.

_____ **5.** Anna thought that her daughter e. get help for his drinking problem.

_____ **6.** Erin wanted her mother to reassure her   f. was a rebellious teenager.

_____ **7.** At the same time, she thought that   g. the way Erin acted towards him.

Exercise C Anna wants to help Erin. Read the suggestions in the chart below. Think about a positive and a negative consequence for each suggestion. Write the consequences in the chart. The first one is done as an example. Add two more suggestions of your own.

Ways to Help Erin

Suggestions	Positive Consequences	Negative Consequences
1. Send Erin to a counselor.	Erin will have an adult to talk to.	Erin may be angry and refuse to talk.
2. Move to a new city.		
3. Take Erin to an Al-Anon meeting.		
4. Convince Erin to report Mark to the police.		
5.		
6.		

Exercise D Write a paragraph about ways to help Erin. Include three suggestions and their consequences from Exercise C. Begin with this sentence: "There are three different ways to help Erin." End your paragraph with this sentence: "If I were Erin's mother, I would _____."

When you finish, read your paragraph. Think about these questions:

- Is the order of the sentences logical?
- Have you included positive and negative consequences for each suggestion?
- Did you add details to make your sentences interesting?
- Have you used words correctly?
- Have you used new words from this unit? Which words?
- Did you check your spelling, punctuation, and capitalization carefully?

In-Class Extension Share your paragraph with your classmates.

Lesson 3 Substance Abuse: Problems and Solutions

Exercise A Add the word endings from the box to the vocabulary words below to make new words. You may use a dictionary. Change spelling when necessary. Write the new words on the lines. Some endings are used more than once. The first word is done as an example.

One Step Up In your notebook, write sentences using the new words.

-al	-ful	-ist	-atory	-ial	-ive

_____behavioral_____ **1.** behavior

_____ **2.** psychology

_____ **3.** protect

_____ **4.** confident

_____ **5.** mandate

_____ **6.** resent

_____ **7.** abuse

Exercise B Unscramble the sentences and write them on the lines. The first sentence is done as an example.

1. substance / symptoms / to recognize / the / abuse / of / Learn

_____Learn to recognize the symptoms of substance abuse._____

2. a / cough / glazed / physical signs / Red / are / eyes / and / lasting

_____

3. irresponsible behavior / depression / Personality and mood changes / emotional signs / and / are

_____

_____

4. from / breaking rules / family / Arguing / are / also / withdrawing / and / signs

_____

_____

5. grades / absences / discipline / problems / many / are / Signs / at school / and / lower

_____

_____

Exercise C Compare how people in the US and in your home country deal with certain issues by completing the chart below.

Issue	In My Home Country	In the US
Child Care	Older family members care for children while parents work.	Paid babysitters care for children while parents work.
Domestic Violence		
Alcoholism		
Smoking		

Some issues listed on the chart may have more than one solution. How similar or different are the two countries?

Which country, in your opinion, has a better approach to dealing with an issue that is important to you? In your notebook, write a paragraph with a topic sentence that states your opinion: "I feel that _____ has a more effective way of dealing with the problem of _____ than _____." Then add two or three sentences that support your point.

In-Class Extension Share your paragraph with your classmates.

Looking at Your Goals Think about your goals for this unit.

How well can you . . .	Not very well		Somewhat		Very well
find resources to help with physical and substance abuse?	1	2	3	4	5
protect yourself from physical and mental abuse?	1	2	3	4	5
solve a problem related to substance abuse?	1	2	3	4	5
communicate well with people who need help?	1	2	3	4	5
talk in English to agencies and other helping resources?	1	2	3	4	5
another goal: _____	1	2	3	4	5

Learning about Problem Solving Think back on the lessons. What was the most important thing you learned about dealing with physical, mental, and substance abuse?

_____

_____

What do you still need to learn about dealing with physical, mental, and substance abuse? List one or two things.

_____

_____

Improving Your English In this unit you studied these areas of English. Check the ones that have improved.

_____ understanding words for offering and asking for help

_____ understanding words for talking about difficult issues

_____ identifying and using prepositions and prepositional phrases

_____ pronouncing *of*

_____ pronouncing words with final consonants held over

_____ taking notes while listening to a conversation

_____ understanding a reading without knowing every word

_____ reading and interpreting information in tables

_____ reading brochures

_____ writing letters or conversations

_____ _____
another thing that you improved

Lesson 1 Becoming Your Own Boss

Exercise A Complete Donna's journal entry with the phrases from the box.

catch	depend on	go for it	write down

Today I watched an interesting interview on TV. Unfortunately, I didn't

have a pen or paper so I couldn't _____ some of the
₁

information. The interview was so fast that I didn't _____
₂

everything. I can't _____ my memory, so I probably
₃

missed some important points. One thing I do remember was the advice to

make your dreams come true: "_____!" I will.
₄

Exercise B Complete the sentences. Write about yourself.

1. I always have to write down _____.

2. I didn't catch what my teacher said when _____.

3. I depend on _____.

4. One thing I recently went for was _____.

Exercise C Write about yourself. Which would you prefer: to work for
yourself or to work for someone else? Why? Give several reasons.

I would prefer to _____
for the following reasons.

a. _____

b. _____

c. _____

I know that I might not like some things about my choice. For

example, _____

_____

_____.

However, I know that with persistence and hard work I will

succeed because _____

_____.

One Step Up
On your own paper write a
paragraph about your choice,
using the outline that you just
made. Show the paragraph to
your teacher.

Exercise D Think about your community.

1. Can you name a small business in your area that failed? _____

2. Can you name a small business that seems successful? _____

3. Give one reason for the success and the failure:

   I believe that one reason _____ is successful is _____

   _____ .

   I believe that one reason _____ was not successful is _____

   _____ .

Exercise E Write a sentence for each word below. Add details about what you like. Use *which, that,* or *who* in your sentences. The first question is done as an example.

1. (people)   _I like people who help others._ _____

2. (films) _____

3. (cars) _____

4. (apartments) _____

Exercise F Rewrite the sentences using the words in parentheses. The first sentence is done as an example.

1. Ralph, the TV interviewer, doesn't like to work at one thing too long. (persistence)

   Ralph, the TV interviewer, does not have a lot of persistence. _____

2. Kim Corby Cooper stopped working and enjoyed her life. (retired)

   _____

3. Her first business placed secretaries to work for short periods of time in businesses. (temporary)

   _____

4. She liked working on her own. (independent)

   _____

5. She had unusual and interesting ideas for her next business. (creative)

   _____

Lesson 2 Doing the Paperwork

Exercise A How many tips for completing an application can you remember from Lesson 2 in the student book? Write a few of them. Here's one example:

1.   *You should make a photocopy of the form.*

2. _____

3. _____

4. _____

Do you have a tip of your own to add? Write it here:

You should _____ .

Exercise B Rewrite the sentences from Exercise A. Give advice about the past. Here is one example:

1.   *You should have made a photocopy of the form.*

2. _____

3. _____

4. _____

Read the sentences aloud, practicing reducing *should have*: "shooduv."

Exercise C Circle the correct words. Then copy the paragraph in your notebook.

   Donna completed an application for a daycare | **1.** value   document   license |. She wanted the | **2.** identification   document   precaution | to be accurate, so she took the | **3.** value   precaution   independence | of checking it many times. It took her several days to complete the | **4.** selfish   independent   detailed | application. She didn't know how to get a tax | **5.** independence   encouragement   identification | number. She had to | **6.** indicate   decision   value | the date when she would begin | **7.** decision   operation   independence | of her business. There were many | **8.** decisions   benefits   documents | to make, and completing the application was very difficult.

Exercise D In your notebook, combine the following sentences using *who, which,* or *that* as a connector. The first one is done as an example.

1. Donna's daycare center opened in September.
   It is very successful.

   _____Donna's daycare center, which opened in September, is very successful._____

2. She took home an application form.
   It was long and complicated.

3. Donna's friend Sheba is the director of a daycare center.
   Sheba works very hard.

4. Donna made a list of safety precautions.
   It was for the fire department.

5. Donna must make a list of people.
   The people live in her home.

6. The back door at Donna's home needs repair.
   It cannot be unlocked.

Exercise E Think of a hero—man or woman—that a classmate talked about in Activity A in the student book or someone else that you admire. Answer the following questions about this person.

1. Who is the hero? _____

2. Where did this person live? _____

3. When did this person live? _____

4. What did the hero do that was special? _____

   _____

5. Give one or two reasons why you admire the hero. _____

   _____

6. What values does the hero have that you respect? _____

   _____

In your notebook, use the answers to write a paragraph about the hero. Your paragraph could start like this:

_____Cesar Chavez is the name of a great hero. He lived in California._____

Lesson 3 Safety First

Exercise A   Read the sentences. In your notebook, rewrite them, changing the order of the clauses. Use correct punctuation. The first one is done as an example.

1. Although parents were supposed to pay on Monday, several did not pay me until Friday.

   Several parents did not pay me until Friday although they were

   supposed to pay on Monday.

2. I should have made a daily schedule so it would be easier to plan activities for the week.

3. Because I didn't go to the library, I didn't have enough books, videos, and puzzles for the children.

4. I should have planned more indoor activities because the weather was cold and rainy.

Exercise B   In your notebook, write three sentences about your day. Follow the example below. Use *although, because,* and *so.*

I passed the vocabulary test because I studied hard.

Exercise C   In the word search puzzle, find the words listed in the box. They can be written forward or backward, across, down, or diagonally. Circle each word. In your notebook, write a sentence using each word.

choke	diagram	hazard	loose	mentor	strict	swallow

```
P  C  H  X  U  F  M  H  N  K  I  G  R  U
O  X  U  S  W  A  L  L  O  W  N  O  Y  H
X  E  Z  E  R  E  D  Z  U  V  T  B  C  R
G  K  S  G  R  E  D  S  L  N  F  H  U  P
B  F  A  O  Y  X  T  P  E  B  L  A  C  K
Y  I  C  J  O  R  F  M  W  N  M  Z  W  K
D  G  F  S  I  L  U  X  R  G  Q  A  J  Q
I  W  J  C  F  L  F  O  F  V  A  R  I  J
O  C  T  C  H  O  K  E  D  U  L  D  B  V
```

Exercise D Before reading the story, fill in the first two columns of the KWL chart below. Then read the story and complete the last column.

Eric Watson had a good idea for a small business. His old dog died, and he missed taking her for walks every day. He didn't want to get a new dog, but he didn't like to walk alone. He noticed many people in his neighborhood had dogs, but he rarely saw the owners walking them.

He decided to research dog-walking businesses on the Internet. There were none in his community. He got encouragement from his wife and friends to try part-time self-employment as a dog walker. He learned how much people paid to have their dogs walked, and he decided how much they should pay him. He thought he could walk two dogs at one time for a half hour. He decided it would be a hazard to try to walk three or four dogs at once.

He liked to walk for a half hour in the morning and again for a half hour in the evening, so he decided he could walk four dogs a day. He made flyers and distributed them in the neighborhood. He included a map of his walking route so customers could see him. Then he waited for calls.

Persistence paid off. By the end of the first month, Eric had four steady customers. He also had a waiting list of 12 more people. Eric had to put an ad in the paper for helpers. Now he has two employees working for him.

What do you **Know** about starting a dog-walking business?	What do you **Want** to know?	What did you **Learn**?

Exercise E Imagine that you want to talk with Eric about his business. You want to find out how he made the business successful. Write questions to ask him. One question has been written as an example.

1. _How much do you charge to walk a dog?_ _____

2. _____

3. _____

4. _____

5. _____

Looking at Your Goals   Think about your goals for this unit.

How well can you . . .	Not very well		Somewhat		Very well
decide if you want to be self-employed?	1	2	3	4	5
identify steps for starting a small business?	1	2	3	4	5
make better decisions?	1	2	3	4	5
check your home and workplace for safety?	1	2	3	4	5
another goal: _____	1	2	3	4	5

Learning about Self-Employment   Think back on the lessons. What was the most important thing you learned about starting a small business and making good decisions?

_____

_____

What do you still need to learn about starting a small business and making good decisions? List one or two things.

_____

_____

Improving Your English   In this unit, you studied these areas of English. Check the ones that have improved.

_____ understanding words about small businesses

_____ understanding safety words

_____ connecting ideas with *so, because,* and *although*

_____ using *who, which,* and *that* in adjective clauses

_____ pronouncing words with the ending *-tion*

_____ pronouncing *could have, should have,* and *would have*

_____ listening for number facts in an interview

_____ understanding and completing a complicated application

_____ relating information in a reading to your own experience

_____ reading an informational article

_____ using a KWL chart as you read

_____ _____
another thing that you improved

Lesson 1 Shopping Smart

Exercise A Match the phrases and their meanings.

_____ **1.** take apart

_____ **2.** come up with

_____ **3.** figure out

_____ **4.** be on a tight budget

_____ **5.** a good deal

a. a bargain

b. not have much money to spend

c. unbuild; disconnect into pieces

d. think about and understand

e. find

Exercise B Complete the sentences.

1. One thing that I know how to take apart is _____

_____.

2. Something I need to figure out about English is _____

_____.

3. I wish that I could come up with _____

_____.

Exercise C Think of some big and small products that you have bought recently. List them in your notebook. Beside each, write the approximate price and whether it was a good deal or a bad one. For each good deal, write how you got that good price. For each bad deal, write what you could have done better.

In-Class Extension Tell your classmates about your purchases, what you paid, and how you could lower the cost of some of them.

Exercise D What do you consider when you buy a product? In the chart below, list four types of products in the first column. Then check the things you consider before you decide to buy. Write any other things you consider in the last column.

Product	Good Price	Good Quality	A Brand I Know	Need the Product	Correct Size	Other Comments
Clothes	✔	✔			✔	the right color

Exercise E Read Bill's journal entry and circle the correct words.

Remember?

A participle is a verb that can be used as an adjective to describe a noun. It can be a present participle (ending in *-ing*) or a past participle (ending in *-ed, -t, -en,* or *-n*).

I was very upset about my | **1.** broke   broken   breaking | camera. My friends gave me a consumer report on digital cameras. They said that it was | **2.** interest   interesting   interested |. They advised me to learn more about this | **3.** fascinating   fascinated   fascinate | technology. At first, I found the reports a little | **4.** overwhelmed   overwhelm   overwhelming |. The technical words seemed | **5.** confused   confusing   confuse |. So many | **6.** surprise   surprised   surprising | facts worried me. But now I am a more | **7.** educating   educated   educate | consumer, and I probably will buy a digital camera rather than a traditional one.

Exercise F Match each word and its definition. Use a dictionary if you need to.

One Step Up
Write a sentence for each word in your notebook. Show your sentences to your teacher.

_____ **1.** bargain   a. good price

_____ **2.** equipment   b. degree of excellence

_____ **3.** purchase   c. promise of quality

_____ **4.** quality   d. buy

_____ **5.** return   e. give back

_____ **6.** warranty   f. tools for work

Exercise G Complete the sentences. Use the words from the box.

budget	consumers	expired	explanation	rate	technical	traditional

1. I'm angry at myself for getting a ticket for an _____ parking meter. I'm on a _____, and I should be more careful.

2. I received a letter from the phone company yesterday. It was an _____ of the _____ increases that _____ would have to pay.

3. I often think that _____ products for the home work better and last longer than the newer and more _____ ones.

Lesson 2 Doing the Research

Exercise A For three minutes, brainstorm a list of things you bought in the last month. Select six items from the list to write in the chart below. Complete the chart.

Product	Why Purchased	Where Purchased	Cost	Were you happy?
1.				
2.				
3.				
4.				
5.				
6.				

Now write two paragraphs in your notebook about the products. Use the information in the chart to add details. Begin the paragraphs with these sentences:

Paragraph 1: "Last month I purchased a _____ , and I was very happy with it."

Paragraph 2: "Last month I also purchased a _____ , and I was very unhappy with it."

In-Class Extension Share your paragraphs with your classmates.

Exercise B Stan is at a department store to return a vacuum cleaner. Number the sentences below to put his conversations in order.

Conversation 1

_____ I don't remember where that is.

_____ Excuse me. Can you tell me where to return a vacuum cleaner?

_____ Go up the escalator and turn right.

_____ Sure. Go to the Service Desk in Appliances.

Conversation 2 (a few minutes later)

_____ No, but I just bought it last week.

_____ I'd like to return this vacuum cleaner.

_____ Here's my card.

_____ If you used a credit card, I can look it up in the computer.

_____ Do you have a store receipt?

Exercise C Read the questions. Use them to write new sentences with embedded questions. The first one is done as an example.

Remember?

Embedded questions are questions within questions.

1. When will this TV go on sale?

   Can you tell me when this TV will go on sale?

One Step Up
In your notebook, write answers to the questions.

2. How long will it take to order this DVD player?

   _____

3. Which model costs the least?

   _____

4. How do these two models compare in performance?

   _____

5. What kind of warranty does this camera come with?

   _____

6. What special features does this TV have?

   _____

Exercise D Match the parts of the sentences. Then write the complete sentences in your notebook.

_____ 1. Before deciding what to buy, Bill needs

_____ 2. When buying a product,

_____ 3. Before you buy, ask about

_____ 4. A consumer report uses a

_____ 5. Some reports have a chart

_____ 6. Do you want your

_____ 7. Many people are

_____ 8. When you write to a company,

a. rating system to rate products.

b. in the same situation.

c. money back?

d. compare the prices.

e. to research cameras.

f. you should describe the problem.

g. that rates products on their quality.

h. a product warranty.

Lesson 3 Consumer Rights and Consumer Awareness

Exercise A Complete the survey about what technology you use in the US and what you used in your home country.

Product	Did you use this in your home country?	If yes, how many?	Do you use this in the US?	If yes, how many?
telephone				
TV				
computer				
e-mail account				
Internet access				
VCR				
DVD player				
CD player				
microwave oven				
Other:				
Other:				

In-Class Extension Use the information to make a class graph of technology use in the US.

Exercise B The following are some things you need to remember when purchasing a product. Complete each sentence with the correct word.

1. Ask friends and family _____ recommendations.

2. Compare prices and get more than _____ estimate.

3. Learn about warranties and compare _____.

4. Make _____ that the product is safe.

5. Read and understand any contract you _____ asked to sign.

6. Make sure that all the blanks are filled _____.

7. Consider paying with a credit _____.

8. Decide _____ advance what you want _____ what you can afford.

Exercise C Look at the chart you made in Exercise A. Write sentences comparing and contrasting your technology use in the US and in your home country. Here is an example:

In the US I have three telephones. In my home country I had one.

_____

_____

_____

_____

_____

_____

_____

Exercise D Use the words in the box to fill in the crossword puzzle. When you finish, write a sentence with each word in your notebook.

| damaged |
| fair |
| fraud |
| illegal |
| improvement |
| inform |
| practice |
| warn |

Across

2. something that is dishonest

4. tell

5. something that is better or makes something better

Down

1. caution

2. balanced; honest

3. hurt; broken

5. against the law

6. usual way of doing something

Looking at Your Goals Think about your goals for this unit.

How well can you . . .	Not very well		Somewhat		Very well
ask good questions before making a purchase?	1	2	3	4	5
use magazines, books, and the Internet to research products?	1	2	3	4	5
get information on products from other people?	1	2	3	4	5
understand English words for rating products?	1	2	3	4	5
another goal: _____	1	2	3	4	5

Learning about Becoming an Educated Consumer Think back on the lessons. What was the most important thing you learned about becoming an educated consumer?

_____

_____

What do you still need to learn about becoming an educated consumer? List one or two things.

_____

_____

Improving Your English In this unit you studied these areas of English. Check the ones that have improved.

_____ understanding words consumers need

_____ using present and past participles as adjectives

_____ asking embedded questions

_____ using correct stress in compound words

_____ using context clues when listening to a conversation

_____ predicting information in a table or chart

_____ reading passages in social studies texts

_____ reading about how to make a consumer complaint

_____ writing about a time you were not happy with a purchase

_____ _____
another thing that you improved

Lesson 1 Read the Fine Print!

Exercise A   Fill in the circle next to the best synonym for each word in the left column. The first one is done as an example. Then write a sentence for each word in your notebook.

1. agreement   Ⓐ oral   Ⓑ pressure   ● contract
2. obligation   Ⓐ right   Ⓑ duty   Ⓒ pressure
3. acknowledge   Ⓐ refuse   Ⓑ accept   Ⓒ question
4. deposit   Ⓐ feature   Ⓑ refund   Ⓒ partial payment
5. rights   Ⓐ fair claims   Ⓑ damages   Ⓒ contracts
6. protect   Ⓐ hurt   Ⓑ discuss   Ⓒ keep safe
7. disappoint   Ⓐ cheat   Ⓑ sadden   Ⓒ deceive
8. legal   Ⓐ lawless   Ⓑ lawful   Ⓒ illegal

Exercise B   Match the dependent and main clauses to make sentences about the story in the lesson. Copy the completed sentences in your notebook.

> **Remember?**
> Use a comma after a dependent clause that starts a sentence.

_____ 1. Before the Wus bought a car,

_____ 2. The salesman should have checked the features of the car

_____ 3. The Wus became angry

_____ 4. After the Wus left the dealership,

_____ 5. Until the car dealer cheated them,

_____ 6. When they returned home without the car or their money,

a. the Wus were disappointed and angry.

b. when the salesman pressured them to take the car anyway.

c. they had never signed a contract without legal advice.

d. before he called the Wus to pick up the car.

e. they learned they had a right to a refund.

f. the Wus had never had legal problems.

Exercise C   Match the five basic parts of a contract and their meanings.

_____ 1. warranty   a. thing for sale

_____ 2. product   b. handwritten name accepting a contract

_____ 3. date of delivery c. promise or guarantee

_____ 4. signature   d. the day the customer will get a product

_____ 5. total price   e. cost

Exercise D   In the contract below, circle and label the five basic parts of a contract that are listed in Exercise C. One part is labeled as an example.

Simon's Sport Shop

479 Bellerose Avenue
Berea, Ohio 26123
Phone: 555-5678

BILL OF SALE

Date of Sale: January 20, 2004   **Customer:** John Smith

Salesperson: Bill Brown   **Address:** 42 South Drive
                                                    Delaware, Ohio 26511

                                         Phone: 555-7541

Merchandise

Product *Products*	Serial #	Price
Homegym Exercise Equipment	867401	$649.00
Weight Set	567922	$288.00
Delivery charge: (includes assembly)		$50.00
Total price:		$987.00

Method of payment: Mastercard # 999 41 7592 2222

Signature: *John Smith* _____   Date *1/20/04*

Date of delivery: January 25, 2004

WARRANTY: Simon's Sport Shop provides no warranty beyond that provided by the manufacturer.

SIMON'S SPORT SHOP EXCHANGE AND RETURN POLICY: Merchandise may be returned within 10 days of delivery. If exchanged or returned, the merchandise must be accompanied by this bill of sale. All exchanges are subject to a 10% restocking charge.

Exercise E   Have you ever been sorry that you signed a contract or made an agreement? Write a paragraph in your notebook about what you would have done differently. If you want, you can use this model:

On _____ I signed a contract that I wish I hadn't. I agreed to _____. I wish I had _____. Next time I sign a contract I will _____.

Lesson 2 Taking Legal Action

Exercise A Was there ever a time when you could have sued someone, but you didn't? Answer the questions below. If you don't have a real incident to write about, you can make one up. Then use your answers to write a paragraph in your notebook.

1. When and where was the incident? _____

2. Who was involved? _____

3. What happened? _____

4. How did you feel at the time? _____

5. Why didn't you sue? _____

6. How do you feel about it now? _____

Exercise B Read these words aloud. Match each word and its meaning. Check the meanings in a dictionary if you are not sure.

_____ **1.** defendant   a. disagreement

_____ **2.** dispute   b. person who sues or makes a complaint

_____ **3.** evidence   c. person who is sued

_____ **4.** hearing   d. facts that support and prove a case

_____ **5.** plaintiff   e. person who saw what happened

_____ **6.** property   f. a legal meeting in court

_____ **7.** witness   g. something a person owns

Exercise C Write definitions for the following words. Then write a sentence for each.

1. (claim) _____

_____

2. (sue) _____

_____

3. (file) _____

_____

4. (support) _____

_____

Exercise D Here's part of the recorded phone message you heard in class.
Complete the message with the words from the box.

claim	defendant	evidence	file	judge	support
Court	dispute	fee	forms	plaintiff	witnesses

Welcome to the City Small Claims _____ information line.
1
Listen to the following information before filing a _____. Press the pound
2
key to have the message repeated.

You can _____ a claim in this court if the amount in
3
_____ is $5,000 or less. The filing _____ is $20. You
4   5
can get claim _____ at the Municipal Building.
6

A Small Claims Court _____ will hear your case. Bring to court any papers,
7
photos, contracts, or other things that _____ your case. You may also bring
8
_____. You—the _____ or the person suing—speak
9   10
first. The _____, or the person you are suing, can also present
11
_____.
12

Exercise E Practice listening. Call an 800 number that has information that you
need. You can get 800 number information by calling 1-800-555-1212.

Listen to the information and answer these questions.

1. How do you replay the message?

_____

2. Is the recording in any language besides English?

_____

3. How do you talk to an operator?

_____

4. What's one thing that you learned from listening to the message?

_____

Lesson 3 Speaking Up for Your Rights

Exercise A Complete the letter with *in, on,* or *at.*

Dear Neighbor:

We would like to inform you that our next meeting will be

_____ February. We will discuss our plan to stop the

1

shopping mall construction in our neighborhood. We plan to meet

_____ 7:30 in the evening _____

2   3

Thursday, the 23rd. Be there and share your ideas for action.

Sincerely,

Citizens for Action

Now think of a community problem you would like to solve. Write a letter to your neighbors asking them to take action.

Exercise B Circle the correct words. Then copy the sentences in your notebook.

1. Mr. and Mrs. Wu | to pressure   pressured   pressuring | the salesman
   for a refund.

2. | Refusing   To refuse   Refused | to get the owner, the salesman
   walked away.

3. Mrs. Wu told her husband | to demand   demanding   demanded |
   to speak to the owner of the dealership.

4. | To file   Filed   Filing | a claim in court was not as difficult as Mr.
   and Mrs. Wu thought it would be.

5. | To sue   Suing   Sued | in Small Claims Court was a positive
   experience for them.

6. Sometimes people must go to court | to settle   settled   settling |
   their disputes.

Exercise C Below is a list of reasons people sign contracts. Add two more reasons to the list if you can.

- to buy or sell a house
- to purchase or sell a car
- to install carpeting
- to make home repairs
- to buy insurance
- to purchase services such as painting, lawn care, cleaning, etc.
- to agree to follow school rules
- _____
- _____

Now change the infinitives to gerunds and write sentences in your notebook:

Buying a house without legal advice is foolish.

Exercise D Here is a list of things to do before you go to court. Decide whether or not to use *the*. If the sentence needs *the*, write it on the line.

> **Remember?**
> General statements leave out articles *a, an,* and *the*.

1. Contact _____ other party to discuss and to try to resolve _____ problem.

2. Learn about _____ Small Claims Court procedures.

3. Determine _____ exact amount in dispute.

4. File _____ claim form and pay _____ filing fee.

5. Prepare for _____ court by organizing your thoughts, collecting evidence, and talking to witnesses.

6. Try to settle the dispute with the other party before _____ hearing.

7. If possible, attend a court hearing in _____ location where your hearing will take place to observe _____ process.

8. Attend _____ hearing and present your case.

Exercise E Mr. Wu prepared for his court day by practicing one sentence. What else could he have done to prepare for that day? Write your suggestions in your notebook.

Looking at Your Goals Think about your goals for this unit.

How well can you . . .	Not very well		Somewhat		Very well
protect your rights?	1	2	3	4	5
understand the language in contracts?	1	2	3	4	5
understand meanings of legal words?	1	2	3	4	5
act appropriately in a courtroom?	1	2	3	4	5
read legal documents?	1	2	3	4	5
another goal: _____	1	2	3	4	5

Learning about Protecting Your Rights Think back on the lessons. What was the most important thing you learned about protecting your rights?

_____

_____

What do you still need to learn about protecting your rights? List one or two things.

_____

_____

Improving Your English In this unit you studied these areas of English. Check the ones that have improved.

_____ understanding and using legal terms

_____ using adverbs of time with past perfect

_____ using prepositions, articles, gerunds, and infinitives

_____ pronouncing consonant blends

_____ reading legal documents

_____ listening to and understanding recorded phone messages

_____ reading stories and articles

_____ writing about service contracts

_____ _____
       another thing that you improved

Lesson 1 Participating in Elections

Exercise A Match the words and their meanings. Write a sentence for each word in your notebook.

_____ **1.** ballot   a. suggested plan

_____ **2.** booth   b. busy, full of energy

_____ **3.** proposal   c. person running for political office

_____ **4.** active   d. private area for voting

_____ **5.** informed   e. run by the people

_____ **6.** candidate   f. list of candidates used for voting

_____ **7.** democratic   g. educated

Exercise B Write the correct form (*-ed* or *-ing*) of the verb in bold type on each line. The first question is done as an example.

1. The political process **interests** Alvin.

He thinks that political speeches are _____*interesting*_____ .

He is _____*interested*_____ in local and national issues.

2. Politics **fascinates** me. I really love to read about elections.

I am _____ by politics.

Politics are _____ to me.

3. Sometimes political speeches **confuse** me.

I am _____ by some political speeches.

Political speeches are sometimes _____ to me.

4. His lack of knowledge of the issues **embarrassed** him.

He was _____ by his lack of knowledge.

His lack of knowledge was _____ to him.

5. The ballot is long and confusing. It **intimidates** Martin.

Martin thinks the ballot is _____ .

Martin is _____ by the ballot.

Exercise C Circle the correct words. Then copy the story in your notebook.

Martin wanted to be an | **1.** inform   informed   informing | voter,

so he listened to speeches and read about | **2.** one candidate

the candidate   the candidates | in the newspaper. He didn't want to

| **3.** waste   wasted   wasting | his vote on Election Day. There was only one

candidate on the | **4.** balloted   balloting   ballot | for his congressional

| **5.** a district   district   the district | . No decision to make there! Martin

didn't like the Republican or | **6.** democracy   democratic   Democratic |

candidate for | **7.** senators   senator   Senator | . He decided to vote for the

third-party candidate. Was he | **8.** waste   wasting   wasted | his vote?

Exercise D Read the words in the list below. Add an ending from the box to each word to make a new word. An ending may be used more than once. Then write a sentence with each new word. The first word is done as an example.

Remember?

You may need to drop the e at the ends of words when you add a new ending.

-tious	-tion	-able	-ative	-ment

1. (participate) __participation__

  __Your participation in this discussion is very important.__

2. (represent) _____

_____

3. (involve) _____

_____

4. (afford) _____

_____

5. (elect) _____

_____

6. (conscience) _____

_____

Lesson 2 Keeping Informed

Exercise A Complete the sentences. Use the correct form and tense of the verb below the line.

After Galina _____ to become a US citizen, she _____
<u>1. decide</u>   <u>2. plan</u>

to take history classes _____ at her English school. She _____
                          <u>3. offer</u>   <u>4. know</u>

some things, but not enough to _____ the citizenship test.
                                 <u>5. take</u>

She had always wanted to _____ in her new country. She
                           <u>6. participate</u>

_____ a lot of research on the Internet, but still she _____
  <u>7. do</u>   <u>8. feel</u>

unprepared for the test. She _____ very little confidence in herself, but once she
                              <u>9. have</u>

_____ the classes she no longer _____ any doubts.
  <u>10. complete</u>   <u>11. have</u>

Exercise B Use the words in the box to fill in the crossword puzzle.

affordable

agency

amend

conscientious

general

regulate

regulation

responsible

services

Across
2. change
3. type of election
6. careful about doing things
8. rule
9. a department of government

Down
1. trustworthy
4. not too expensive
5. control
7. help or assistance

Exercise C Unscramble the sentences. The first one is done as an example.

1. roles and responsibilities / state, / local / National, / different / governments / and / have

   <u>National, state, and local governments have different roles</u>

   <u>and responsibilities.</u>

2. the Constitution / governments / of / national and state / roles and responsibilities / The / by / are defined

   _____

   _____

3. traffic and parking / responsibility / local government / Making / the / is / of / rules

   _____

   _____

4. government / responsibility / Declaring / the / of / the / is / war / federal

   _____

   _____

Exercise D Read the ballot instructions. Circle the errors on the ballot. Write sentences about the errors in your notebook. One sentence is written as an example.

General Election Instructions

1. To vote for a candidate whose name is printed on the ballot, completely fill in the oval next to the name of the candidate.

2. To vote for a candidate whose name is not printed on the ballot, write or stamp the name on the blank line and fill in the oval next to "Write-In Candidate."

3. Any other mark or writing made on the ballot outside the voting ovals will void this ballot.

2005 General Elections

Mayor Vote for one.

◉ Mark Siegel   ✔○ Kathryn Colon

○ Fernando Garcia   ○ Write-In Candidate: _____

<u>The oval for Mark Siegel is only partly filled in.</u>

Lesson 3 Getting Involved

Exercise A How do people in the US and in your home country resolve issues that affect their communities or nation? Write three paragraphs on this question:

- **Step 1** Before you write, use the overlapping circles below to jot down main points about each country. Write points that apply to both countries in the space where the two circles overlap.

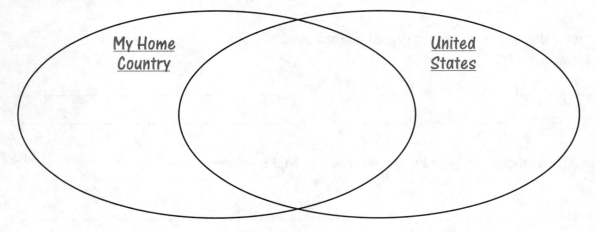

My Home
Country

United
States

- **Step 2** Organize your ideas under two categories:

My Home Country   **United States**

Main Points: _____   Main Points: _____

Supporting Details: _____   Supporting Details: _____

- **Step 3** Use your notes from Step 2 to write one paragraph about your home country and one about the US.

- **Step 4** Write a summary in a third paragraph. Use the information from the overlapping center of the two circles.

Exercise B Here are some steps you could use to create a grassroots organization. Add two more steps of your own. Then number the steps to show the order in which you would do them.

_____ Schedule a meeting to discuss the issue.

_____ Discuss the pros and cons of the solutions.

_____ Identify an issue or problem.

_____ Ask newpapers to print articles about the issues and actions.

_____ Identify other people who are concerned about the problem.

_____ Identify possible solutions to the problem.

_____ your step: _____

_____ your step: _____

Exercise C Complete the paragraph with the words from the box.

civic	grassroots	overcrowding	resolved	shortage

Concerned citizens in Oak Ridge met to discuss two issues. One was the

_____ of affordable housing in their community. The
₁

other issue was _____ in the schools. The citizens were
₂

_____ to find solutions to both issues. One person
₃

suggested that the community look into Houses for the People, a

_____ movement to build affordable homes. Another
₄

person suggested that parents attend the next school board meeting. The

concerned citizens of Oak Ridge really take their _____
₅

responsibilities seriously.

Exercise D As you read this paragraph from a citizenship textbook, underline the past participles.

> The role of the federal government was defined in the
> US Constitution. The government was organized with a system of
> checks and balances. The power was balanced among three
> branches: the legislative branch, the executive branch, and the
> judicial branch. If one branch of government tried to go too far,
> another branch could *check* it, or hold it back. The founders had
> wanted to be sure that no part of the government would have too
> much power. They had lived with the unchecked rule of the
> English king. Therefore, they had been careful to create a
> government with shared power.

One Step Up
Do you know the roles of the three branches of government mentioned in the paragraph? If you are not sure, look them up in an encyclopedia.

Exercise E One word has been reduced in each sentence below. Write the full form of the word on the line. The first one has been done as an example. Then read the sentences aloud.

_he_ **1.** What candidate did e vote for?

_____ **2.** I've seen er on TV.

_____ **3.** Did you hear im at the Civic Center?

_____ **4.** Where did you put is application?

_____ **5.** I don't know where e stands on the issues.

Looking at Your Goals Think about your goals for this unit.

How well can you . . .	Not very well		Somewhat		Very well
understand local, state, and national issues?	1	2	3	4	5
understand how to become more active in your community?	1	2	3	4	5
understand the role of a responsible citizen?	1	2	3	4	5
use the language necessary to keep informed?	1	2	3	4	5
communicate with your government representatives?	1	2	3	4	5
another goal: _____	1	2	3	4	5

Learning about the US Democratic Process Think back on the lessons.
What was the most important thing you learned about the US democratic process?

_____

_____

What do you still need to learn about the US democratic process? List one or
two things.

_____

_____

Improving Your English In this unit you studied these areas of English. Check
the ones that have improved.

_____ understanding words for participating in a democracy

_____ using present and past participles as adjectives

_____ using past participles with regular and irregular verbs

_____ pronouncing and understanding English words with the disappearing *h*

_____ relating what you already know to new information in a reading

_____ reading and understanding an election ballot

_____ listening to discussion at a community meeting

_____ reading and writing about becoming a US citizen

_____ _____
<small>another thing that you improved</small>

Lesson 1 What Works Best for You?

Exercise A Fill in the circle next to the best synonym for each term in the left column. Then write a sentence for each vocabulary term in your notebook.

1. express	Ⓐ speak about	Ⓑ make better	Ⓒ come closer
2. improve	Ⓐ move	Ⓑ speak about	Ⓒ make better
3. course	Ⓐ feature	Ⓑ class	Ⓒ product
4. speech	Ⓐ a talk	Ⓑ an argument	Ⓒ a scream
5. wedding	Ⓐ marriage ceremony	Ⓑ anniversary	Ⓒ engagement
6. approach	Ⓐ bragging	Ⓑ way of standing	Ⓒ way of doing things
7. CD	Ⓐ control date	Ⓑ compact disk	Ⓒ cash deposit
8. convenient	Ⓐ easy	Ⓑ hard	Ⓒ cheap

Exercise B Read the steps for making a decision.

• **Step 1** Think about a decision that you need to make. It could be a big one (Do I move to another state or stay here?) or a small one (Do we see a movie or watch a game on Saturday?). Describe the decision in a complete sentence.

_____

_____

• **Step 2** Read the following list of things to think about when making a decision. Add your own item to the list.

_____ Cost

_____ Schedule

_____ Location

_____ How I feel about it

_____ _____

• **Step 3** Rank the items from Step 2 in order of importance to you. (1 is most important, 5 is least important.)

• **Step 4** Evaluate the items you listed. Write a sentence about your decision.

I may decide to _____

because _____ .

Exercise C Read this story about a diamond robbery. Then complete the sentences with the correct verb form to tell what people were doing when the diamond was taken. The first one is done as an example.

Last Tuesday at 6:30 P.M. two people entered the Museum of Natural History and walked out with the world's largest diamond.

1. The night guard _____was driving_____ to work.
                      drive

2. The day guard _____ to a visitor.
                    talk

3. The museum president _____ a newspaper in her private office.
                    read

4. A woman and two children _____ juice in the museum cafeteria.
                    drink

Remember?

Use a singular verb with a singular subject:
One **man was** talking.
Two **men were** talking.

Exercise D Read the two poems.

While I Was Walking to Work . . .
Two bluebirds were singing,
A bell was ringing,
My love was calling,
The rain was falling.

While I Was Walking to Work . . .
A vendor was selling,
My boss was yelling,
A car was passing,
My friends were laughing.

Now, write a poem in your notebook. Use *while* and the past continuous. Begin with one of these clauses, or write your own: "While I was sleeping . . ."; "While I was working . . ."; "While I was talking to you . . .".

Exercise E Complete the sentences with the words from the box.

convenience	convenient	course	multimedia	online

1. Antonia is thinking about taking a _____ in photography.

2. She is trying to find a course that is at a _____ time and location.

3. She is considering a _____ course because she likes to use a computer.

4. Antonia likes the _____ of studying _____.

Lesson 2 Working Out the Details

Exercise A Practice active listening at home. Ask a friend or family member a good question and really listen to the answer. Try to listen for at least two full minutes. To review active listening, look at page 115 in your student book.

Ask one of these questions, or ask your own question.

- Do you think older people or younger people are better students? Why?
- Tell me about an unhappy experience you had in school. What did you learn from the unhappy experience?
- Tell me about the best teacher you had. What made that person a good teacher for you?

Exercise B Write about what happened when you did Exercise A.

1. How did the person feel about your active listening? Ask. Be specific. Was the person happy? Surprised? Did he or she feel important?

_____

_____

2. How did it feel to listen actively? Were you nervous? Was it difficult or easy to listen well to the speaker for two minutes or more? Do you think you could use active listening often? If so, when and where? If not, why not?

_____

_____

_____

Exercise C Match each word and its meaning. Then write a sentence in your notebook using each word.

_____ **1.** outdo   a. able to speak a language easily

_____ **2.** preview   b. to get the wrong idea

_____ **3.** misunderstand   c. to see in advance

_____ **4.** mentally   d. the length of a life

_____ **5.** continuing   e. related to the mind

_____ **6.** fluent   f. going on for a long time

_____ **7.** lifelong   g. to do more or better than

Exercise D Make new words by adding prefixes to the root words. Write the new word on the line. The first word is done as an example. Write the meanings of the new words in your notebook. Use a dictionary if you need to.

One Step Up
Write two more words with each prefix in your notebook. Check the words in a dictionary.

pre- (meaning: before)

view   _preview_

caution   _____

pay   _____

out- (meaning: beyond, further, greater)

live   _____

run   _____

do   _____

re- (meaning: to do again)

write   _____

consider   _____

view   _____

in- (meaning: not)

secure   _____

expensive   _____

complete   _____

mis- (meaning: wrong, opposite)

place   _____

understand   _____

spell   _____

Exercise E Add suffixes to the root words to make new words. The first word is done as an example. Check the spelling in a dictionary.

One Step Up
Write three more words with each suffix in your notebook. Check the words in a dictionary.

-ly (meaning: in the manner; how)

active   _actively_

mental   _____

continual   _____

-er (meaning: person who does)

arrange   _____

interview   _____

work   _____

Lesson 3 Showing Your Pride

Exercise A Unscramble the sentences and write them on the lines. Use correct capitalization and punctuation. The first sentence is done as an example.

1. information / four steps / active learning / when / Follow / you / to / for / read

   Follow four steps to active learning when you read for information.

2. for / skim / main points / First / article / the / looking / the

   _____

3. and examples / the article / support / those / Read / more details / again / to find / main points / more slowly / that

   _____

   _____

4. the / points / Summarize / yourself / writing / article / by / the / for / most important

   _____

   _____

5. the / questions / Evaluate / by asking / yourself / points

   _____

Exercise B Write sentences about people who have changed their minds. Use the verbs in parentheses in this form: *had been* + verb + *-ing* + *to* + simple verb. The first word is done as an example.

1. (sleep) _I had been planning to sleep with the window open._

   I changed my mind when it rained.

2. (call) _____

   _____

3. (buy) _____

   _____

4. (refuse) _____

   _____

5. (give) _____

   _____

Exercise C Complete the paragraph with the words from the box. Then copy the paragraph in your notebook.

express	guest	lifelong	memorable	relationship	speech

I was a _____ recently at a 50th anniversary
⟨1⟩

party. My _____ with the anniversary couple
⟨2⟩

began more than 36 years ago when I was a university student.

Bill was a professor who could _____ himself
⟨3⟩

well. He once gave a powerful _____ about
⟨4⟩

learning styles. Over the years, I have often thought about his

_____ words about learning. He was a wonderful
⟨5⟩

professor who later, along with his wife, became a

_____ friend to me.
⟨6⟩

One Step Up
Rewrite the paragraph using past continuous forms of the verbs.

Exercise D Think about your school experiences in the US and in your home country. How have they been similar? How have they been different? Fill in the diagram below.

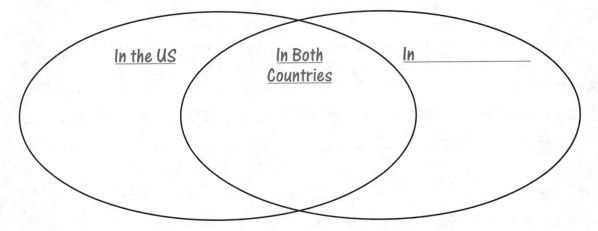

In the US   In Both   In _____
                   Countries

Use the information in the diagram to write a paragraph comparing and contrasting school experiences in the US and in your home country. Write the paragraph in your notebook.

In-Class Extension Share your paragraph with your classmates.

Looking at Your Goals Think back on your goals for this unit.

How well can you . . .	Not very well		Somewhat		Very well
use ways to study better?	1	2	3	4	5
understand different styles of learning?	1	2	3	4	5
understand your personal learning style?	1	2	3	4	5
use your personal learning style to learn better?	1	2	3	4	5
understand different approaches to learning?	1	2	3	4	5
another goal: _____	1	2	3	4	5

Learning about Learning Styles Think back on the lessons. What was the most important thing you learned about learning styles and approaches to learning?

_____

_____

What do you still need to learn about learning styles and approaches to learning? List one or two things.

_____

_____

Improving Your English In this unit you studied these areas of English. Check the ones that have improved.

_____ using words for giving a speech

_____ talking about ways to learn

_____ using the past continuous

_____ using the past perfect continuous

_____ pronouncing and understanding English words with disappearing sounds and syllables

_____ reading the yellow pages to find resources

_____ using active listening

_____ looking for parallel structures when reading a speech

_____ reading and writing about learning styles

_____ _____
another thing that you improved

Lesson 1 Making the Most of Yourself

Exercise A Fill in the circle next to the best synonym for each word in the left column.

1. advancement	Ⓐ moving ahead	Ⓑ agency	Ⓒ studying
2. characteristic	Ⓐ image	Ⓑ feature	Ⓒ skill
3. effort	Ⓐ success	Ⓑ appearance	Ⓒ hard work
4. image	Ⓐ chance	Ⓑ appearance	Ⓒ trial
5. obstacle	Ⓐ barrier	Ⓑ failure	Ⓒ help
6. possibility	Ⓐ no chance	Ⓑ chance	Ⓒ wish
7. develop	Ⓐ build	Ⓑ learn	Ⓒ solve

Exercise B Think about the best and worst jobs, paid or unpaid, that you have had.
Write notes in the chart below.

	Best Job	Worst Job
Who was the employer?		
What was your job?		
When and where was it?		
What were your hours?		
What was your pay?		
What were your duties?		
What training did you have?		
What kind of people did you work with?		
What did you think of your boss?		

Use your notes to write a paragraph about your best or worst job. Use this topic
sentence as a model or write one of your own.

My best/worst job was in _____ when I worked at _____.

In-Class Extension Share your paragraph with your classmates.

Exercise C Complete the conversation with the words from the box. Add two more lines of your own. Use as many vocabulary words from the unit as you can from the unit list on page 75.

background	effort	employment	overqualified	reliable

Ramon: So Mariana, how's your _____ search going?
₁

Mariana: Not very well. I've been told repeatedly that I am _____
₂
for the jobs that I have applied for.

Ramon: I'm sure that with your _____ and a little more
₃
_____ you will find the right job.
₄

Mariana: I hope so! I know I'm _____, and I work hard.
₅

Ramon: _____

Mariana: _____

Exercise D Combine a word from the box with each word below to make a compound word. Write the compound word on the line. The first one has been done as an example.

One Step Up
Write a list of other compound words that you know.

-book	-ground	✔-room	-roots	-stand	-work

_____classroom_____ **1.** class-

_____ **2.** grass-

_____ **3.** check-

_____ **4.** home-

_____ **5.** back-

_____ **6.** news-

Exercise E Read this description of jobs at Cleaning Crews, Inc. Rewrite the description in your notebook, changing the verbs to present passive. The first sentence has been rewritten as an example.

We offer competitive pay and benefits. We hire ambitious people. We offer a flexible schedule to each employee. We check your background and references. We train you. We develop your skills.

Competitive pay and benefits are offered.

Lesson 2 Making Your Work History Count

Exercise A Use the words in the box to describe the personal characteristics of the people in the sentences. The first sentence is done as an example.

✔assertive	hard-working	optimistic	persevering
eager to learn	high-achieving	organized	self-reliant

1. Joan isn't afraid to speak about her ideas or opinions. She is _____assertive_____.

2. Marta's desk is always in order. She is _____.

3. Elias is hopeful, and he sees life in a positive way. He is _____.

4. Yolanda doesn't give up when there are obstacles in her way. She is _____.

5. Sean often succeeds without asking anyone for help. He is _____.

6. Teresa does more than her employer expects. She is _____.

7. Rocio works long hours at her nursing job. She is _____.

8. Boris likes learning new things. He is _____.

Exercise B Read this list of jobs. Decide what personal characteristic is the most important for each. Use the words from this unit or other words you know. You can use the word lists on pages 67–75.

1. (US President) _____

2. (doctor) _____

3. (food server) _____

4. (housekeeper) _____

5. (police officer) _____

6. (packer) _____

7. (teacher) _____

8. (car salesperson) _____

9. (carpenter) _____

10. (cashier) _____

11. (firefighter) _____

12. (mail carrier) _____

13. (assembler) _____

14. (computer programmer) _____

One Step Up
Which personal qualities do you have? Write a few sentences about the qualities you need for your job.

Exercise C Complete the sentences with the passive form of the verb below the line. The first sentence is done as an example.

1. At the meeting, everyone <u>was surprised</u> by the
   surprise
   treasurer's report.

2. People _____ that the money in the budget was
   amaze
   spent so fast.

3. They asked many questions about the way money _____.
   spend

4. Treasurers usually _____ to save money for associations.
   train

5. After the meeting, the treasurer _____ to be more careful.
   order

6. This year's expenses and income _____ to last year's.
   compare

Exercise D How do you define success? Is success in the US the same as success in your home country? Compare and contrast success in the two countries. Write notes in the chart below.

One Step Up Make a list of people who are successful. In your notebook, write a sentence or two about each person, explaining what makes that person successful.

Success in the US	Success in My Home Country

Use your notes to write an essay about success. Use the sentences below to help you organize the paragraphs in your essay if you need help.

Success means different things to different people. In the US, I think success means _____. In my home country, _____, success means _____. To me, success means _____. I will know that I am successful when _____.

In-Class Extension Share your essay with your classmates.

Lesson 3 Making a Good Impression

Exercise A Read Jana's journal entry about a recent job interview. Circle the correct words. Then copy the entry in your notebook.

One Step Up Write a journal entry about a job interview that you have had. Use as many vocabulary words from the unit as you can. Underline the words.

Wednesday, October 16

Today I finally had the interview for the job of my dreams. I was very [**1.** concerning   concerned   concern] about it, and I had problems sleeping last night. Although my experience as an office manager is [**2.** limiting   limit   limited], I tried to show how [**3.** competent   competence   compete] I am. The interviewer asked me [**4.** specify   specified   to specify] how I would act in certain difficult situations. She said that she [**5.** appreciate   appreciating   appreciated] the way I said I would give [**6.** criticize   criticized   criticism] to an employee. The friendly, relaxed atmosphere of the interview [**7.** impressive   impressed   impress] me. I hope that the interviewer liked me as much as I liked her!

Exercise B Read these job interview questions. Underline the verbs. Write the verb tense on the line. The first question is done as an example.

One Step Up
In your notebook, write answers to the questions. Use complete sentences.

simple past (both verbs)   **1.** How old <u>were</u> you when you <u>started</u> your first job?

_____   **2.** How long will you stay with the company?

_____   **3.** How long have you been looking for another job?

_____   **4.** What things about the job interest you most?

_____   **5.** Can we check your references?

_____   **6.** What will your marital status be in the future?

_____   **7.** Are you planning to have a family?

_____   **8.** How old are you?

_____   **9.** Have you ever had a conflict on a job?

_____   **10.** Why should we hire you?

Exercise C Some of the questions in Exercise B are illegal. Write *L* for *Legal* and
I for *Illegal* next to each question.

_____ **1.** How old were you when you started your first job?

_____ **2.** How long will you stay with the company?

_____ **3.** How long have you been looking for another job?

_____ **4.** What things about the job interest you most?

_____ **5.** Can we check your references?

_____ **6.** What will your marital status be in the future?

_____ **7.** Are you planning to have a family?

_____ **8.** How old are you?

_____ **9.** Have you ever had a conflict on a job?

_____ **10.** Why should we hire you?

Exercise D Answer the questions.

1. Have you ever been asked illegal interview questions? If so, what questions?

_____

2. How did you respond to the illegal questions?

_____

3. Were you offered the job? Did you accept it? Explain what happened.

_____

Exercise E Think of a response to the interview questions below.

1. Do you think people find it difficult to work for a woman?

_____

2. Are you planning to have a family?

_____

3. Do you expect to be paid for overtime work?

_____

4. Who will take care of your children when they are sick?

_____

Looking at Your Goals Think about your goals for this unit.

How well can you . . .	Not very well		Somewhat		Very well
develop your employment skills?	1	2	3	4	5
spend more time with your family or having fun?	1	2	3	4	5
continue your education?	1	2	3	4	5
do service in a community or religious group?	1	2	3	4	5
another goal: _____	1	2	3	4	5

Learning about Finding a Good Job Think back on the lessons. What was
the most important thing you learned about preparing for a job interview and doing
your resume?

_____

_____

What do you still need to learn about job interviews and resumes? List one or
two things.

_____

_____

Improving Your English In this unit you studied these areas of English. Check
the ones that have improved.

_____ using resume and job interview words

_____ using the present passive tense

_____ using verb tenses correctly

_____ pronouncing diphthongs correctly

_____ using correct syllable stress

_____ reading job announcements critically

_____ analyzing job skills and experiences

_____ listening to and answering job interview
questions

_____ reading and writing career advice

_____ _____
another thing that you improved

Grammar Talk: Comparing Simple Past with Present Perfect

Simple Past	Present Perfect
Grandmother's husband **gave** her a music box.	Grandmother **has listened** to the music for 50 years.
Patria **studied** hard in high school.	Patria **has dreamed** of going to college since then.

Compare the simple past sentences with the present perfect sentences. How are the verbs different? Which verbs talk about something that happened at a specific time in the past? Which talk about something that happened at an unspecified time or times in the past and is continuing? What verb form is used with have *or* has *in the present perfect?*

Grammar Talk: Comparing Present Perfect and Past Perfect

Present Perfect	Past Perfect
I **have learned** that mistakes are necessary in life.	I **had made** many mistakes before I dared to ask for help.
He **has accomplished** his goal.	He **had accomplished** his goal before he came to the US.
They **have worked** here for six weeks.	I **had worked** for six weeks when my boss called me into his office.

Compare the present perfect sentences with the past perfect sentences. Think about when the action takes place. The present perfect sentences show action occurring at an indefinite time in the past or action that continues on into the present. The past perfect sentences show action completed before another event in the past.

Vocabulary

These are the words that you learned in Unit 1.

- accomplish
- achieve
- appropriate
- aptitude
- career
- clarify
- dare
- details
- dream
- event
- experience
- frustrated
- fulfill
- imagine
- long-term goals
- personality
- potential
- predict
- prediction
- profession
- reality
- short-term goals
- stick
- stuck
- success
- successful

Vocabulary

These are the words that you learned in Unit 2.

- ability
- achievement
- advertise
- advice
- annoyed
- body language
- brag
- challenge
- confused
- custom
- embarrassed
- formal
- informal
- network
- professional
- resume
- shy
- shyness
- situation
- skill
- suggestion
- talent
- tense
- tone
- worried
- worry

Grammar Talk: Conditional Contrary to Fact

If I **were** rich, I **would sing** all day. *OR*
I **would sing** all day if I **were** rich.

If he **had** time, he **would deal with** the problem. *OR*
He **would deal with** the problem if he **had** time.

Look at the verb tenses in the main clauses and the if clauses.

Did you notice that in each sentence, the order of the main clause and the if clause can be reversed?

Did you notice that the sentences all tell about possibilities, not facts? They are contrary-to-fact sentences. The verb in the main clause in each sentence is the conditional (would + base form). The verb in the if clause is in the past tense.

Grammar Talk: Indirect Speech

Direct:	Hassam said,	"I **want** to take **my** paintings to the shop."
Indirect:	Present:	Hassam **says** that he **wants** to take **his** paintings to the shop
	Past:	Hassam **said** that he **wanted** to take **his** paintings to the shop.

When do you use indirect speech? What happens to the verb and the pronoun when the sentence changes from direct to indirect speech? Look at the extra punctuation marks in the direct speech sentence. What are they? Why are they used?

Grammar Talk: Prepositions and Their Objects

A prepositional phrase is a preposition followed by a noun (and its modifiers) or a pronoun. The noun or the pronoun is the object of the preposition.

Preposition	Noun/Pronoun	Preposition	Noun
during	the break	at	work, home
about	her daughter's boyfriend	before	church
of	them	by	bus, train, car, boat
on	the job	for	years and years
with	my friend	in	Paris, jail

Grammar Talk: Adjective and Adverb Prepositional Phrases

Adjective Phrases	Adverb Phrases
Erin's boyfriend is the man **on the right.**	Erin hoped **for a peaceful discussion.**
She is the girl **in the bedroom**.	Anna needs to be patient **with her daughter.**
Erin's car is the one **with a punctured tire.**	They fought endlessly, **without any results.**

The phrases above modify nouns or pronouns. They answer these questions:
Which *man is Erin's boyfriend?*
Who *is she?*
Which *car has the punctured tire?*

The phrases above modify verbs, adjectives, or adverbs. They answer these questions:
What *did Erin hope for?*
Who *should Anna be patient with?*
How *did they fight?*

Vocabulary

These are the words that you learned in Unit 3.

abuse
abusive
accuse
agency
barrier
behavior
clinic
communicate
confidential
confront
cope
counseling
counselor
dilemma
encourage
ignore
issue
mandatory
monitor
protection
protective
psychologist
reassure
rebellious
resentful
resource
strategy
substance abuse
terrified
therapy
violence
violent
voluntary

Grammar Talk: Adjective Clauses with *Who, Which,* and *That*

Adjectives	Adjective Clauses
Sheba is an **Ethiopian** woman.	Sheba is a woman **who comes from Ethiopia.**
The Pizza Place is a **successful** business.	The Pizza Place, **which is always busy,** is a successful business.
The **locked** exit door needs repair.	The exit **that is near the kitchen** was locked.

An adjective is a word that describes or gives more information about a noun. An adjective clause is a group of words with a subject and verb that does the same thing—describes a noun or gives more information about a noun.

Who refers to people. Which *refers to things.* That *can refer to people or things.* That *and* which *have different uses.*

Grammar Talk: Connecting Ideas with *So, Because,* and *Although*

Simple	Combined
Donna washes her hands a lot. The children are healthier.	**Because Donna washes her hands a lot,** the children are healthier.
Donna washes her hands often. Some children get colds.	**Although Donna washes her hands often, s**ome children get colds.
I vacuum the rug. Children with allergies are more comfortable.	I vacuum the rug, **so children with allergies are more comfortable.**

A complex sentence has one clause that is an independent sentence and one clause that is dependent. Dependent clauses start with words that show relationships, for example, because *or* although. *A compound sentence has two independent clauses joined with a coordinating conjunction that also shows relationships, for example,* so.

Vocabulary

These are the words that you learned in Unit 4.

- benefits
- breakable
- choke
- cooperation
- creative
- decision
- detailed
- diagram
- document
- encouragement
- hazard
- identification
- independence
- independent
- indicate
- license
- loose
- mentor
- operation
- opportunity
- persistence
- precaution
- retired
- security
- self-employed
- selfish
- strict
- swallow
- temporary
- unbreakable
- value

Grammar Talk: Present and Past Participles Used as Adjectives

Read the sentences in each column. Notice the two endings, -ed and -ing, on the words in bold type.

The camera instructions were **confusing** Bill even more.	The **confusing** instructions did not help him.
Bill had **assembled** the pieces of the camera.	Some of the **assembled** pieces were broken.

Words that end in -ing are present participles. Words that end in -ed are past participles. Can you see that in the sentences in the left column, these words show action? The present and past participles are parts of the verbs in those sentences. In the sentences in the right column, the same words are used to describe objects. In those sentences, the participles are used as adjectives to describe nouns or pronouns.

The past participles of most irregular verbs also are irregular. Those forms do not end in -ed, and they must be memorized.

Grammar Talk: Embedded Questions

Will you tell me **who broke the camera?**	Do you know **when this item will go on sale?**
Can you show me **how you do it?**	Do you know **how long this is going to take?**

Embedded means "included inside of." Notice the embedded questions in bold type inside the longer questions above. What do you notice about the word order? In the first sentence, the word order is the same as in all other who questions. What happens to the word order in the other three sentences?

Vocabulary

These are the words that you learned in Unit 5.

bargain
budget
consumer
damaged
digital
equipment
expired
explanation
fair
feature
fraud
high quality
illegal
improvement
inform
low quality
model
performance
practice
product
purchase
rate
rating
research
return
score
source
technical
technology
traditional
warn
warranty

Vocabulary

These are the words that you learned in Unit 6.

- agreement
- anxious
- binding
- cheat
- claim
- contract
- court
- defendant
- demand
- deposit
- disappointed
- dispute
- evidence
- file
- hearing
- judge
- legal
- obligation
- patient
- persistent
- plaintiff
- pressure
- property
- protect
- refund
- refuse
- rights
- settle
- sue
- support
- witness

Grammar Talk: Adverbs of Time with the Past Perfect

Main Clause with Past Perfect Verb	Dependent Clause with Adverb of Time
She **had read** the contract	**before** she signed it.
He had taken her to court	**when** she refused to pay.
They **had accused** the dealer	**after** he cheated them.
I **hadn't gone** to court	**until** I saw that there was no other way.

Read each main clause in the left column and the dependent clause in the right column. What happened first in each pair of clauses, the action in the left column or in the right column?

Grammar Talk: Choosing and Using Difficult Language Forms

Choosing and Using Prepositions of Time: *On, In,* **and** *At*

You are scheduled to appear in court **on June 21, 2002.**

Your hearing is **at 3 p.m.**

The judge's decision will be mailed to you **in February.**

The prepositions in, on, *and* at *are very exact for each time expression. So if you need to use a month, you must say or write* in. *If you say or write a complete or specific date, use* on.

Choosing and Using Articles: *A/An, The,* and No Article	Choosing and Using Gerunds and Infinitives
Nonspecific	*Used as a noun (gerund)*
• You need to sign **an** agreement.	• **Winning** this case is important to Mr. Wu.
• You need to fill out **a** form.	• **Suing** the dealer is the only way to get his money back.
General	*Following a verb (infinitive)*
• People go to court to settle disputes.	• Mr. Wu wants **to win** the case.
Specific	• He will have **to sue** the dealer.
• A form is available at **the** courthouse.	

Grammar Talk: Present and Past Participles as Adjectives

Notice that the verbs in the sentences on the left are "verbs of emotion." See how they change when they are turned into adjectives.

Galina was **excited** by the elections.	The elections were **exciting** to Galina.
She was **confused** by the proposal on the ballot.	The proposal on the ballot was **confusing.**

*The past participle of a verb (verb + -ed or irregular form) and the present participle (verb + -ing) can be used as adjectives. The past participle tells how someone feels: "I am **fascinated** by the American political process." Fascinated says how I feel about the American political process. "The American political process is **fascinating** to me." The present participle, fascinating, describes something that will make someone feel fascinated.*

What happens to the verb when the subject of the sentence experiences the emotion? What happens to the verb when the subject does not experience the emotion?

Grammar Talk: Past Participle of Irregular Verbs

Look at the past participles of irregular verbs in these sentences.

One of the voting machines was **broken.**
Have you **heard** about the new agency to help immigrants?
Galina hadn't **read** the proposal before she went to the polling place.
Our teacher had **done** a lot of research before she voted.
The candidate for mayor was well **known** in her district.

Can you identify the structures in which past participles are used? What is the main verb for each of these past participles?

Vocabulary

These are the words that you learned in Unit 7.

active
affordable
amend
amendment
ballot
booth
candidate
civic
conscientious
democratic
district
election
embarrassed/embarrassing
fascinated/fascinating
general election
grassroots
housing project
informed
intimidated/intimidating
involved
low income
overcrowded
overcrowding
participate
proposal
regulate
regulation
representative
resolve
responsibility
responsible
senator
services
shortage
town council
waste

Grammar Talk: Past Continuous

Willie felt nervous.

His wife and daughter **were planning** the wedding.

Willie felt nervous **when** his wife and daughter **were planning** the wedding.

I **was studying.**

My wife called some schools.

While I **was studying,** my wife called some schools.

We **were taking** the test from 9:00 to 10:00.

Sara arrived at 9:30.

When we **were taking** the test, Sara arrived.

The simple past indicates an action that started and ended at a specific time in the past (last night, yesterday, in 2002).

The past continuous tells about an event that was happening at the same time as another event in the past.

Notice that the clauses in past continuous sentences can be in different orders.

When and while are time words that are often used with the past continuous. What is the difference between these two words?

Grammar Talk: Past Perfect Continuous

You **had been worrying** about your speech.

We **had been trying** to pass the citizenship test.

The teacher **had been looking** for a chance to work with adult learners.

The past perfect continuous is used to talk about something that had been happening for some time in the past. What three verb forms are used in this tense?

Vocabulary

These are the words that you learned in Unit 8.

- actively
- approach
- compact disk (CD)
- continuing
- convenience
- convenient
- course
- decide
- distance learning
- express
- fluent
- guest
- improve
- insecure
- lifelong
- memorable
- mentally
- misunderstand
- multimedia
- online
- outdo
- powerful
- preview
- pride
- private
- reconsider
- relationship
- speech
- wedding

Grammar Talk: Passive Voice in Simple Present

Active	Passive
Mega Corporation **employs** many people.	Many people **are employed** by Mega Corporation.
The mail carrier **delivers** the packages.	The packages **are delivered** by the mail carrier.
People in the Bahamas **speak** English.	English **is spoken** by people in the Bahamas.

The subject in an active sentence becomes the object of a preposition in a passive sentence.

The passive voice in simple present is formed with a present tense form of the verb be (am, is, *or* are) + *past participle.*

Vocabulary

These are the words that you learned in Unit 9.

- advancement
- ambitious
- appreciate
- assertive
- background
- characteristic
- competent
- concern
- criticism
- develop
- duty
- eager to learn
- effort
- employment
- flexible
- hard-working
- high-achieving
- honest
- image
- impressed
- limited
- obstacle
- optimistic
- organized
- overcome
- overqualified
- permit
- persevering
- possibility
- reference
- reliable
- secure
- self-reliant
- specify
- train
- trustworthy

Grammar Talk: Verb Tense Review

This chart reviews six verb tenses that are often used.

	Affirmative Statement	**Negative Statement**	**Question**
Simple Present	I **am** concerned about it.	He **is not** trustworthy.	**Are** they competent?
	Martha **wants** a job.	Ana **doesn't like** criticism.	**Do** you **react** well to criticism?
Present Progressive	I**'m being** optimistic.	Ray **is not being** helpful.	**Are** you **being** assertive?
	We**'re looking** for a job.	Joe **is not talking** about his job.	**Are** they **preparing** a budget?
Be + Going to + verb	He**'s going to be** treasurer.	The effort **is not going to be** worth it.	**Are** there **going to be** obstacles?
	They**'re going to vote** for a chairperson.	He**'s not going to succeed.**	**Are** you **going to face** them?
Simple Past	Possibilities **were** good.	Lila **wasn't** overqualified.	**Was** your mother a single parent?
	He **developed** his best characteristics.	They **didn't offer** many benefits.	**Did** she **list** her references?
Future	I **will be** responsible for the duties.	She **will not be** an assertive candidate.	**Will** these children **be** optimistic and self-reliant?
	Now Tuan **will earn** a good living.	Their situation **will not help** them get more aid.	**Will** you **receive** the message by snail mail?
Present Perfect	As workers, they **have been** eager to learn.	I **haven't been** lonely here without you.	**Have** you **been** to this agency before?
	This year, **I've trained** six people in this company.	Carol **hasn't used** her car for weeks now.	**Have** you **stated** which kind of work you want?
Past Perfect	Amy **had been** sick.	Martha **hadn't been** optimistic about the job.	**Had** the personnel department **been** fair?
	I **had traveled** in South America during those years.	My parents **hadn't arrived** in the US in 1975.	**Had** the brothers **attained** high-level jobs?

Answer Key

UNIT 1
Lesson 1

Exercise A
3. has learned
4. came
5. has accomplished
6. imagined
7. achieved or has achieved

Exercise C
2. c 3. e 4. a 5. b

Exercise D
2. no information
3. He has dreamed of discovering a cure for the common cold since he was 10 years old.
4. He has read over 500 books about the common cold.
5. He has asked a famous botanist for information about herbs and natural medicine.

Lesson 2

Exercise B
Simple past: had, was, wondered, tried, remembered, wanted, didn't dare, found, said, called, heard, told, went, learned, did
Present perfect: I've told, has helped, have had
Past perfect: had run, hadn't seen, had quit, I'd worked

Lesson 3

Exercise A
2. O 3. O 4. F 5. O

Exercise B

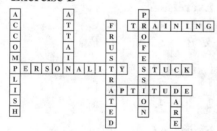

UNIT 2
Lesson 1

Exercise C
2. skills 5. professional
3. network 6. challenge
4. advice

Exercise D
2. If I had more time, I could make these photos look more professional.
3. So do you think they would look better if I added a little color to the photos?

Exercise E
2. network 5. skills
3. worry 6. tone
4. shyness

Exercise F
2. a 3. d 4. b
2. I would improve my pronunciation if I watched more TV in English.
3. If I listened to the advice of other people, I would make fewer mistakes.
4. I wouldn't feel tense in social situations if I understood customs in the US.

Lesson 2

Exercise B
1. just in time
2. make a good impression
3. how to handle
4. go well
5. in the eye

Lesson 3

Exercise C
Indirect speech:
I asked her to tell Ms. Patterson that I was there.
I asked her if she wanted to see some pictures of my work.
(She) said that we should sit down first.
I asked how she liked the weather.
She asked if I had a resume and pictures.
She said that my work was excellent and well-organized.
Direct speech:
I said, "Tell Ms. Patterson that I'm here."
I asked, "Do you want to see some pictures of my work?"
She said, "We should sit down first."
I asked, "How do you like the weather?"
She asked, "Do you have a resume and pictures?"
She said, "Your work is excellent and well-organized."

Exercise D

UNIT 3
Lesson 1

Exercise A
1. dilemma   8. ignore
2. strategy   9. barriers
3. communicating 10. protection
4. confront   11. resource
5. abusive   12. issues
6. violent   13. neglect
7. cope

Exercise B
2. at/in
3. for/with, in/at
4. during/with
5. in, on
6. next
7. for, on
8. with
9. to/with, in, for

Exercise D
1. b 2. c 3. a

Answer Key

Exercise E
1. give up
2. lose control
3. pay attention

Lesson 2

Exercise B
1. c   3. g   5. f   7. b
2. e   4. a   6. d

Lesson 3

Exercise A
2. psychologist   5. mandatory
3. protective   6. resentful
4. confidential   7. abusive

Exercise B
2. Red, glazed eyes and a lasting cough are physical signs.
3. Personality and mood changes, irresponsible behavior, and depression are emotional signs.
4. Arguing, breaking rules, and withdrawing from family are also signs.
5. Signs at school are lower grades, many absences, and discipline problems.

UNIT 4
Lesson 1

Exercise A
1. write down   3. depend on
2. catch   4. Go for it

Exercise F
2. Kim Corby Cooper retired.
3. Her first business placed temporary secretaries in businesses.
4. She liked being independent.
5. She had creative ideas for her next business.

Lesson 2

Exercise C
1. license   5. identification
2. document   6. indicate
3. precaution   7. operation
4. detailed   8. decisions

Exercise D
2. She took home an application form that was long and complicated.
3. Donna's friend Sheba, who works very hard, is the director of a daycare center.
4. Donna made a list of safety precautions that was for the fire department.
5. Donna must make a list of the people who live in her home.
6. The back door at Donna's home, which cannot be unlocked, needs repair.

Lesson 3

Exercise A
2. So it would be easier to plan activities for the week, I should have made a daily schedule.
3. I didn't have enough books, videos, and puzzles for the children because I didn't go to the library.
4. Because the weather was cold and rainy, I should have planned more indoor activities.

Exercise C

```
P C H X U F M H N K I G R U
O X U S W A L L O W N O Y H
X E Z E R E D Z U V T B C R
G K S G R E D S L N F H U P
B F A O Y X T P E B L A C K
Y I C J O R F M W N M Z W K
D G F S I L U X R G Q A J Q
I W J C F L F O F V A R I J
O C T C H O K E D U L D B V
```

UNIT 5
Lesson 1

Exercise A
1. c   2. e   3. d   4. b   5. a

Exercise E
1. broken   5. confusing
2. interesting   6. surprising
3. fascinating   7. educated
4. overwhelming

Exercise F
1. a   3. d   5. e
2. f   4. b   6. c

Exercise G
1. expired, budget
2. explanation, rate, consumers
3. traditional, technical

Lesson 2

Exercise B
Conversation 1
3, 1, 4, 2
Conversation 2
3, 1, 5, 4, 2

Exercise D
1. e   3. h   5. g   7. b
2. d   4. a   6. c   8. f

Lesson 3

Exercise B
1. for   4. sure   7. card
2. one   5. are   8. in, and
3. them   6. in

Exercise D

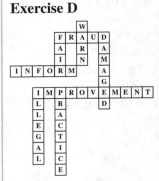

UNIT 6
Lesson 1

Exercise A
2. B   4. C   6. C   8. B
3. B   5. A   7. B

Exercise B
1. c   3. b   5. f
2. d   4. e   6. a

Exercise C
1. c   3. d   5. e
2. a   4. b

Answer Key

Exercise D
Total price: $987
Signature: John Smith
Date of delivery: January 25, 2004
Warranty: Simon's Sports Shop provides no warranty beyond that provided by the manufacturer.

Lesson 2

Exercise B
1. c   3. d   5. b   7. e
2. a   4. f   6. g

Exercise D
1. Court
2. claim
3. file
4. dispute
5. fee
6. forms
7. judge
8. support
9. witnesses
10. plaintiff
11. defendant
12. evidence

Lesson 3

Exercise A
1. in   2. at   3. on

Exercise B
1. pressured
2. Refusing
3. to demand
4. Filing
5. Suing
6. to settle

Exercise D
1. the, the
2. the
3. the
4. the, the
5. (no *the*)
6. the
7. the, the
8. the

UNIT 7
Lesson 1

Exercise A
1. f   3. a   5. g   7. e
2. d   4. b   6. c

Exercise B
2. fascinated, fascinating
3. confused, confusing
4. embarrassed, embarrassing
5. intimidating, intimidated

Exercise C
1. informed
2. the candidates
3. waste
4. ballot
5. district
6. Democratic
7. senator
8. wasting

Exercise D
2. representative
3. involvement
4. affordable
5. election or electable
6. conscientious

Lesson 2

Exercise A
1. decided
2. planned
3. offered
4. knew
5. take
6. participate
7. did
8. felt
9. had
10. completed
11. had

Exercise B

Exercise C
2. The roles and responsibilities of national and state governments are defined by the Constitution.
3. Making traffic and parking rules is the responsibility of local government.
4. Declaring war is the responsibility of the federal government.

Lesson 3

Exercise C
1. shortage
2. overcrowding
3. resolved
4. grassroots
5. civic

Exercise D
defined, organized, balanced, wanted, lived, unchecked, been, shared

Exercise E
2. her   3. him   4. his   5. he

UNIT 8
Lesson 1

Exercise A
1. A   3. B   5. A   7. B
2. C   4. A   6. C   8. A

Exercise C
2. was talking
3. was reading
4. were drinking

Exercise E
1. course
2. convenient
3. multimedia
4. convenience, online

Lesson 2

Exercise C
1. g   3. b   5. f   7. d
2. c   4. e   6. a

Exercise D
precaution, prepay
rewrite, reconsider, review
misplace, misunderstand, misspell
outlive, outrun, outdo
insecure, inexpensive, incomplete

Exercise E
mentally, continually
arranger, interviewer, worker

Lesson 3

Exercise A
2. First, skim the article looking for the main points.
3. Read the article again more slowly to find more details and examples that support those main points.
4. Summarize the article for yourself by writing the most important points.
5. Evaluate the points by asking yourself questions.

Answer Key

Exercise C
1. guest
2. relationship
3. express
4. speech
5. memorable
6. lifelong

UNIT 9
Lesson 1

Exercise A
1. A 3. C 5. A 7. A
2. B 4. B 6. B

Exercise C
1. employment 4. effort
2. overqualified 5. reliable
3. background

Exercise D
2. grassroots 5. background
3. checkbook 6. newsstand
4. homework

Exercise E
Ambitious people are hired by us. A flexible schedule is offered to each employee. Your background and references are checked. You are trained. Your skills are developed.

Lesson 2

Exercise A
2. organized 6. high-achieving
3. optimistic 7. hard-working
4. persevering 8. eager to learn
5. self-reliant

Exercise C
2. were amazed
3. was spent
4. are trained
5. was ordered
6. were compared

Lesson 3

Exercise A
1. concerned 5. appreciated
2. limited 6. criticism
3. competent 7. impressed
4. to specify

Exercise B
2. will stay, future
3. have been looking, present perfect progressive
4. interest, present
5. can check, present
6. will be, future
7. are planning, present progressive
8. are, present
9. have had, present perfect
10. should hire, present

Exercise C
1. L 6. I
2. L 7. I
3. L 8. I
4. L 9. L
5. L 10. L